SCHOLASTIC

GRADE
2

Literary Passages:
Close Reading

Marcia Miller & Martin Lee

D0814234

NEW YORK • TORONTO • LONDON • AUCKLA
MEXICO CITY • NEW DELHI • HONG KONG • BUENOS AIRES

Cover design: Tannaz Fassihi
Cover illustration: Patrick George
Interior design: Kathy Massaro
Interior illustrations by Anne Kennedy, except page 14 by Robert W. Alley

"Up the Elephant's Trunk" from *Playful Poems That Build Reading Skills* © 2000 by Kirk Mann. Used by permission of Scholastic Inc.

ISBN: 978-0-545-79385-8
Copyright © 2016 by Scholastic Inc.
All rights reserved.
Printed in the U.S.A.
Published by Scholastic Inc.

2 3 4 5 6 7 8 9 10   40   23 22 21 20 19 18 17 16

Contents

....
: Literary Text Passages :
....

Character

Point of View

Setting/Mood

Key Events & Details

Sequence of Events

Problem & Solution

Context Clues

Compare & Contrast

Introduction

Reading, discussing, and sharing literary texts contributes greatly to the development of well-rounded minds. Exposure to diverse literary genres, characters, and plots, set in varied time periods and cultures, models for readers how the world works. Literary texts help us learn how people explore, interact, struggle, grow, and solve problems. In short, reading fiction enriches us.

Modern science supports that the human brain is hard-wired for stories. All cultures immerse their children in stories that explain the ways of the world while engaging their emotions. Although many students enjoy reading fiction, navigating the wide variety of rich literary texts poses challenges for evolving readers. Students may lack sufficient vocabulary or background knowledge to follow the material, and some genres may be unfamiliar at first. This is why exposing students more frequently to complex literary texts and introducing them to active reading-comprehension strategies are now key components of successful reading instruction. Useful strategies, clearly taught, can empower readers to approach literary texts purposefully, closely, and independently. Such active tools provide students with a foundation for success not only in school, but for the rest of their lives.

> **Connections to the Standards**
>
> The chart on page 9 details how the lessons in this book will help your students meet the more rigorous demands of today's reading standards for literature.

Text Marking: A Powerful Active-Reading Strategy

To improve their comprehension of complex literary texts, students must actively engage with the text. Careful and consistent text marking by hand is one valuable way to accomplish this. To begin with, by numbering paragraphs, students can readily identify the location of useful narrative details when discussing a passage. By circling main characters, underlining pertinent clues to setting or sequence, and boxing key vocabulary, students interact directly with the material, making it more digestible in the process. But the true goal of teaching text marking is to help students internalize an effective close-reading strategy, not to have them show how many marks they can make on a page.

Purposeful text marking intensifies a reader's focus. It helps readers identify narrative elements as they read, and recognize and isolate key details or connect relevant ideas presented in the text. For instance, boxing words like *first, then, next,* and *finally* can clarify the sequence of ideas or events in a passage. When students are asked to compare and contrast elements in a passage, signal words, such as *both, but,* or *however,* can make identifying similarities and differences more apparent. Words like *trouble, plan,* and *idea* serve as clues to finding problems and their solutions. Furthermore, the physical act of writing by hand, in itself, helps students not only process what they read, but remember it as well.

About the Passages

The 20 reproducible passages in this book, which vary in genres, topics, purposes, tones, and tasks, address eight key reading-comprehension skills, from identifying character, settings, and key events and details, to sequencing and finding problem-solution relationships. Consult the table of contents to see the scope of skills, genres, content areas, and Lexile scores of the passages. (The poem on page 22 does not include a Lexile score because poetry is excluded from Lexile measurements.) The Lexile scores fall within the ranges recommended for second graders. (The scores for grade 2, revised to reflect the more rigorous demands of today's higher standards, range from 380 to 650. This range addresses the variety commonly seen in typical second grade classrooms.)

Each passage appears on its own page, beginning with the title, the genre or topic, and the main comprehension skill the passage addresses. The passages include illustrations as visual elements, as well as typical text elements, such as words in capital letters and boldface type.

The passages are organized to help scaffold young students' understanding of each comprehension skill. For example, in the first passage of the section on sequence of events, students identify and number three important events as well as three key signal words and phrases. The next passage has them identify and number the important events and four signal words. In the last passage, students identify the important events and recognize pertinent signal words on their own.

Depending on the abilities of your students, and until they are reading independently, the passages will work best as shared reading activities using an interactive whiteboard or document camera, or during guided reading so that you can support readers. If you do assign passages to individuals, pairs, small groups, or the entire class, it's a good idea to preview each passage before you assign it, to ensure that your students have the skills needed to complete it successfully. (See the next page for a close-reading routine to model for students.)

Reading-Comprehension Question Pages

Following each passage is a reproducible "Do More" page of text-dependent comprehension questions: two are multiple-choice questions that call for a single response and a brief, text-based explanation to justify that choice. The other two questions are open-response items. The questions address a range of comprehension strategies and skills. All questions share the goal of ensuring that students engage in close reading of the text, grasp its key ideas, and provide text-based evidence to support their answers. Keep additional paper on hand so students have ample space to write complete and thorough answers.

An answer key (pages 54–63) includes annotated versions of each marked passage and sample answers to its related questions. Maintain flexibility in assessing student responses, as some markings and answers to open-response questions may vary. (Since students are likely to mark different places in the text for particular skills, the annotated versions in the answer key highlight a variety of possible responses.) Encourage students to self-assess and revise their answers as you review the text markings together. This approach encourages discussion, comparison, extension, reinforcement, and correlation to other reading skills.

Teaching Routine for Close Reading and Purposeful Text Marking

Any text can become more accessible to readers once they have learned to bring various strategies, such as purposeful text marking, to the reading process. Here is one suggested routine that may be effective in your classroom.

Preview

- **Engage prior knowledge** of the topic of the passage and its genre. Help students link it to similar topics or examples of the genre they may have read.

- **Identify the reading skill** for which students will be marking the text. Display or distribute the Comprehension Skill Summary Card that applies to the passage. Go over its key ideas. (See Comprehension Skill Summary Cards, page 8, for more.)

Model *(for the first passage, to familiarize students with the process)*

- **Display the passage**, using an interactive whiteboard, document camera, or other resource, and provide students with their own copy. Preview the text with students by having them read the title and look at the illustration.

- **Draw attention to the markings** students will use to enhance their understanding of the passage. Link the text marking box to the Comprehension Skill Summary Card for clarification.

- **Read aloud the passage** as students follow along. Guide students to think about the featured skill and to note any questions they may have on sticky-notes.

- **Mark the text together.** Begin by numbering the paragraphs. Then discuss the choices you make when marking the text, demonstrating and explaining how various text elements support the skill. Check that students understand how to mark the text using the icons and graphics shown in the text marking box.

Read

- **Display each passage for a shared reading experience.** Do a quick-read of the passage together to familiarize students with it. Then read it together a second time, pausing as necessary to answer questions, draw connections, or clarify words. Then read the passage once more, this time with an eye to the features described in the text marking box.

- **Invite students to offer ideas for additional markings.** These might include noting unfamiliar vocabulary, an idiom or phrase they may not understand, or an especially interesting, unusual, or important detail they want to remember. Model how to use sticky-notes, colored pencils, highlighters, question marks, or check marks.

Respond

- **If students are able, have them read the passage independently.** This reading is intended to allow students to mark the text themselves, with your support, as needed. It will also prepare them to discuss the passage and offer their views about it.

- **Have students answer the questions** on the companion Do More page. Depending on the abilities of your students, you might read aloud the questions, and then have them answer orally. Model how to look back at the text markings and other text evidence for assistance. This will help students provide complete and supported responses.

Literary Passages: Close Reading (Grade 2)
© 2016 Scholastic Inc.

Comprehension Skill Summary Cards

To help students review the eight reading-comprehension skills this book addresses and the specific terms associated with each, have them use the reproducible Comprehension Skill Summary Cards (pages 10–13). The boldface terms on each card are the same ones students will identify as they mark the text.

You might duplicate, cut out, and distribute a particular Comprehension Skill Summary Card before assigning a passage that focuses on that skill. Discuss the elements of the skill together to ensure that students fully grasp it. Encourage students to save and collect the cards, which they can use as a set of reading aids to refer to whenever they read any type of literary text. Or display the cards in a reading center in your classroom, where they will be available at all times.

Tips and Suggestions

- The text-marking process is versatile and adaptable. While numbering, boxing, circling, and underlining are the most common methods, you can personalize the strategy for your class if it helps augment the process. You might have students use letters to mark text; they can, for example, write MC to indicate a main character, D to mark a detail, or P for problem and S for solution. Whichever technique you use, focus on the need for consistency of marking.

- You may wish to extend the text-marking strategy by having students identify other aspects of writing, such as figurative language or confusing words, expressions or idioms.

Comprehension Skill

Character

Characters are who a story is about. A character can be a person, an animal, or a thing.

- Read for details that describe each character.

- Read for details that describe different characters so you can tell them apart.

- Read for details that tell if and how characters change or learn during the story.

Comprehension Skill

Point of View

The **point of view** of a story means who is telling it.
What you learn in the story comes through that point of view.

- Some stories are told by a **narrator**. The narrator can be someone who is not in the story.
  Look for words like **he**, **she**, and **they**.

  The narrator can be a character in the story.
  Look for words like **I** and **me**.

- Point of view also helps you understand how characters think and feel.

- One way to tell a character's point of view is by what he or she says.

Comprehension Skill

Compare & Contrast

Authors may describe how people, places, things, or ideas are **alike** and **different**.

- To **compare** means to tell how things are the same or alike.

- To **contrast** means to tell how things are different.

- **Signal words** give clues that help you compare and contrast.

Examples for comparing: **both, too, like, also,** and **in the same way**.

Examples for contrasting: **but, only, however, unlike,** and **different**.

Literary Passages: Close Reading (Grade 2)
© 2016 Scholastic Inc.

Connections to the Standards

The lessons in this book support the College and Career Readiness Anchor Standards for Reading for students in grades K–12. These broad standards, which serve as the basis of many state standards, were developed to establish rigorous educational expectations with the goal of providing students nationwide with a quality education that prepares them for college and careers. The chart below details how the lessons align with specific reading standards for literary texts for students in grade 2.

These materials also address language standards, including skills in the conventions of standard English, knowledge of language, and vocabulary acquisition and use. In addition, students meet writing standards as they answer questions about the passages, demonstrating their ability to convey ideas coherently, clearly, and with support from the text.

Reading Standards for Literature	Passages
Key Ideas and Details	
• Ask and answer such questions as *who, what, where, when, why,* and *how* to demonstrate understanding of key details in a text.	1–20
• Recount stories, including fables and folktales from diverse cultures, and determine their central message, lesson, or moral.	2–5, 7, 10, 12, 15–18, 20
• Describe how characters in a story respond to major events and challenges.	1–18, 20
Craft and Structure	
• Describe how words and phrases (e.g., regular beats, alliteration, rhymes, repeated lines) supply rhythm and meaning in a story, poem, or song.	1, 3–11, 13–20
• Describe the overall structure of a story, including describing how the beginning introduces the story and the ending concludes the action.	1–20
• Acknowledge differences in the points of view of characters, including by speaking in a different voice for each character when reading dialogue aloud.	1–8, 12, 14, 16, 17
Integration of Knowledge and Ideas	
• Use information gained from the illustrations and words in a print or digital text to demonstrate understanding of its characters, setting, or plot.	1–20
Range of Reading and Level of Text Complexity	
• By the end of the year, read and comprehend literature, including stories and poetry, in the grades 2–3 text complexity band proficiently, with scaffolding as needed at the high end of the range.	1–20

Literary Passages: Close Reading (Grade 2)
© 2016 Scholastic Inc.

Point of View

The **point of view** of a story means who is telling it. What you learn in the story comes through that point of view.

- Some stories are told by a **narrator**. The narrator can be someone who is not in the story. Look for words like **he, she**, and **they**.

- The narrator can be a character in the story. Look for words like **I** and **me**.

- Point of view also helps you understand how characters think and feel.

- One way to tell a character's point of view is by what he or she says.

Character

Characters are who a story is about. A character can be a person, an animal, or a thing.

- Read for details that describe each character.

- Read for details that describe different characters so you can tell them apart.

- Read for details that tell if and how characters change or learn during the story.

Key Events & Details

Things happen in every story. **Events** are actions or things that happen. Events move the story along.

Some events are more important than others.

- A **key event** answers the question "What is an important thing that happens?"

- **Details** tell more about a key event.

Setting/Mood

The **setting** of a story tells where and when the story takes place. The setting can help create the **mood** or feeling of the story.

- Read for details that tell where a story takes place.

  It can be a **real** place.

  It can be a **make-believe** place.

- Read for details that tell when the story takes place.

  It might be set in the **present** (now).

  It might be set in the **past** (long ago).

  It might be set in the **future** (years from now).

- Think about how the setting helps you feel the mood of the story.

Literary Passages: Close Reading (Grade 2)
© 2016 Scholastic Inc.

Problem & Solution

Sometimes you will read about **problems** and how they get **solved**.

- A **problem** is a kind of trouble or puzzle.
  A problem needs to be fixed or solved.

- A **solution** is how to solve a problem.
  A solution makes things better.

- **Signal words** are clues to a problem and its solutions.

  Examples for problems: **question, need,** and **trouble.**

  Examples for solutions: **answer, idea, result, plan, reason,** and **solve.**

Sequence of Events

When you read, look for the **order** in which things happen.

- **Events** are actions or things that happen in a story.

- The **sequence** is the order in which events happen.

- **Signal words** give clues about the sequence of events.

  Examples: **before, first, second, next, then, now, later, after, finally,** and **last,** as well as **dates** and **times.**

Literary Passages: Close Reading (Grade 2)
© 2016 Scholastic Inc.

Compare & Contrast

Authors may describe how people, places, things, or ideas are **alike** and **different**.

- To **compare** means to tell how things are the same or alike.

- To **contrast** means to tell how things are different.

- **Signal words** give clues that help you compare and contrast.

Examples for comparing: **both, too, like, also**, and **in the same way**.

Examples for contrasting: **but, only, however, unlike**, and **different**.

Context Clues

Authors may use words you don't know. Other words nearby may help.

- **Context** means all the words and sentences around a word you don't know.

- **Context clues** are hints that can help you figure out the meaning of a word.

Look for words that mean the same or opposite.

Use details to help you understand the word.

Name _____   Date _____

Dancing Day

Read the dance story.

Then follow the directions in the Text Marking box.

Zoey was walking home from school with her friend Trey. She had an extra bounce in her step.

"Why are you so jiggly and bubbly today?" asked Trey.

"It's Wednesday," said Zoey. "This is my favorite day. It's when I go to my dance class. My friend Max's mom teaches us. She used to be a dancer. We practice in their basement."

She gave her backpack to Trey to hold. Then she did a graceful leap and twirl right there in the middle of the sidewalk. Trey smiled, gave her a "thumbs up," and said, "Look at you, girl!"

"Why don't you come along with me," she said. "It's really fun to dance!"

Text Marking

Think about the story.

◯   Circle WHO the story is mostly about.

_____   Underline two details that tell about that person.

Name _____   Date _____

Dancing Day

▶ **Answer each question. Give details from the story.**

1 Which shows that Trey noticed "an extra bounce" in Zoey's step?

○ A. He held her school bag.

○ B. He smiled and gave a "thumbs up."

○ C. He asked why she was jiggly and bubbly.

○ D. He didn't notice anything different about Zoey.

What helped you answer? _____

_____

_____

2 Who said, "She used to be a dancer"?

○ A. Trey   ○ B. Zoey   ○ C. Max's mom   ○ D. Max

What helped you answer? _____

_____

_____

3 Why do you think Zoey danced for Trey? _____

_____

_____

4 Do you think Trey will go with Zoey to her dance class? Why or why not?

_____

_____

_____

Satellite Search

Read the historical fiction story.
Then follow the directions in the Text Marking box.

It was October, 1957. Nora and Fred went to bed early because they would lose sleep later. Fred fussed about the babyish bedtime. Fred didn't care about science. Nora was different. She knew about Sputnik (SPUHT-nik). She knew it was the first satellite (SAT-uh-lite) ever to travel around Earth. She had heard this spacecraft's "beep-beep" sound on the radio. She saw photos and read news stories about it.

Sputnik was about the size of a beach ball.

Text Marking

Think about the kids in the story.

◯ Circle the names of these two characters.

_____ Underline one detail about each character.

That night, the whole family went outside after midnight. They searched the dark sky for Sputnik. "Is that it?" Nora asked, pointing to a bright star.

"No," said Dad. "Sputnik moves fast, like a shooting star."

"Can't I go to sleep?" whined Fred.

"No! Keep looking!" Nora urged.

Mom spotted it first, pointing, "I think that's Sputnik!

"Freddie, look!" cried Nora. But her brother was already sound asleep on the grass.

Satellite Search

▶ **Answer each question. Give details from the story.**

1 What was Sputnik?

     ○ A. a beach ball   ○ C. a small satellite

     ○ B. a shooting star   ○ D. another word for midnight

What helped you answer? _____

_____

_____

2 Which best describes Nora?

     ○ A. She is interested in science.   ○ C. She is a bossy person.

     ○ B. She has trouble sleeping.   ○ D. She has good luck.

What helped you answer? _____

_____

_____

3 Why did Nora and Fred go to sleep early that night?

_____

_____

_____

4 How do you know that this story took place in the past?

_____

_____

_____

Literary Passages: Close Reading (Grade 2)
© 2016 Scholastic Inc.

Fox and Stork

Read the fable.

Then follow the directions in the Text Marking box.

One day Fox made soup. As it cooked, Stork flew by. That gave Fox a sly idea. He invited Stork to join him for soup. "Come back at dark, Stork."

"How kind," Stork thought. But Fox planned a mean trick.

Later, Fox served bowls of soup. But Stork's bowl was too shallow for her long beak. She could not taste one drop. Fox slurped loudly and said, "Mmmm, yummy!" Poor Stork felt hungry and insulted. Still, she asked Fox to eat with her the next night. Fox agreed.

Fox went to Stork's home for dinner. Stork served fish stew in tall skinny jars. Stork's pointy beak fit nicely, and she ate her fill. But Fox could not taste one drop. He went home hungry and angry.

Text Marking

Think about the fable.

◯   Circle the name of each character.

_____   Underline two details about each character.

Literary Passages: Close Reading (Grade 2)
© 2016 Scholastic Inc.

Fox and Stork

▶ **Answer each question. Give details from the fable.**

1 What reason did Fox have to invite Stork to dinner?

   ○ A. He wanted to play a trick on Stork.

   ○ B. He had made too much soup.

   ○ C. He knew she was hungry.

   ○ D. He didn't like to eat dinner by himself.

   What helped you answer? _____

   _____

2 Which is the moral of this story?

   ○ A. It is not wise to be too greedy.

   ○ B. Birds of a feather flock together.

   ○ C. Whatever you do, do it with all your might.

   ○ D. If you play tricks on others, expect them to be played on you.

   What helped you answer? _____

   _____

3 Why couldn't Fox eat the stew Stork made?

   _____

   _____

4 Why did Fox slurp loudly and say, "Mmmm, yummy"?

   _____

   _____

Literary Passages: Close Reading (Grade 2)
© 2016 Scholastic Inc.

Bart's Spider Scare

Read the nature story.

Then follow the directions in the Text Marking box.

Bart was in the garden when he spotted a scary, hairy spider. He began shouting, "A spider, a spider! Kill it quick!"

"Calm down," called Grandpa from the porch. "What's all the **fuss**?"

Bart told Grandpa about the spider. He led Grandpa to the garden for a look.

"Now that is a welcome sight," said Grandpa. "This spider will eat insects that could harm my plants, so I'm glad it's here." Then he said, "Welcome to my garden, spider!"

"But...I thought spiders were bad," said Bart. "Don't they bite? Don't they have poison?"

> ### ★ Text Marking ★
>
> Think about the point of view of the characters. How do they react to the spider in different ways?
>
> ▭   Draw a box around each character's name.
>
> ◯   Circle words that the first character says.
>
> _____   Underline words that the other character says.

"Some spiders can hurt people, but many are helpful," said Grandpa. "It pays to learn about nature. Then you will know which animals to stay away from. You will also know a friend when you spot one!"

Bart's Spider Scare

▶ **Answer each question. Give details from the story.**

1 What word does NOT mean the same as **fuss**?

○ A. excitement   ○ B. trouble   ○ C. quiet   ○ D. worrying

What helped you answer? _____

_____

_____

2 What clues help you tell when each character is talking?

○ A. question marks (**?**)   ○ C. periods (.)

○ B. commas (,)   ○ D. quotation marks (" ")

What helped you answer? _____

_____

_____

3 Why did Grandpa call the spider "a welcome sight"?

_____

_____

4 Bart and Grandpa have different points of view about the spider. Explain how the story shows this.

_____

_____

_____

_____

Up the Elephant's Trunk

by Kirk Mann

Read the poem.

Then follow the directions in the Text Marking box.

The elephant once said to me,

"Mouse, please climb in my nose

And go until I say to stop,

Then scratch there with your toes."

I climbed inside the long, deep trunk,

The air was damp and gray.

I walked across some peanut shells

And grass and bits of hay.

Then halfway up the bumpy trail

The elephant yelled, "Stop!"

"Scratch," he said, "with all your might,

And jump and kick and hop."

I scratched and itched and itched and scratched.

He finally yelled, "Enough!"

And then he blew me out his trunk

With lots of other stuff!

★ Text Marking

Each character in the poem has a point of view.

☐   Draw a box around the narrator.

◯   Circle the character that wants help.

___   Underline what the narrator does to help.

Name _____   Date _____

Up the Elephant's Trunk

▶ **Answer each question. Give details from the poem.**

1 What is the elephant's problem?

○ A. He is afraid of the mouse. ○ C. He can't jump, kick, or hop.

○ B. He has an itch he can't reach. ○ D. The air in his trunk is too damp.

What helped you answer? _____

_____

_____

2 Where is the mouse for most of the poem?

○ A. on the elephant's trunk ○ C. far from the elephant's trunk

○ B. on a trail beside the elephant ○ D. inside the elephant's trunk

What helped you answer? _____

_____

_____

3 What does "the bumpy trail" describe?

_____

_____

4 Think about the mouse. What can you say about its character?

_____

_____

_____

Literary Passages: Close Reading (Grade 2)
© 2016 Scholastic Inc.

Name _____ Date _____

Waterfall of Light

Read the holiday story.

Then follow the directions in the Text Marking box.

Shun Park was crowded with excited people. They stood in groups or sat on folding chairs or benches. The cold night sky was filled with stars. Soon it would be filled with brighter, more colorful stars—Chinese New Year fireworks. I could hardly wait!

"Have some noodles, Ming," my dad said. But I was too excited to eat. Then the fireworks started.

First came a loud "BOOM," then a whistling noise. Red, orange, and gold fireworks lit up the night. Sparks showered down. They looked like a waterfall of light. Everyone gazed up at the sky. People clapped and cried, "Oooh!" and "Ahhh!" Then, with one last "BOOM!" three, four, five fireworks went up at once. The sky exploded with color. Happy New Year!

Text Marking

Think about the setting and mood of the story.

☐	Draw a box around WHEN the story takes place.
⬯	Circle WHERE the story takes place.
___	<u>Underline</u> two details that set the mood.

Name _____   Date _____

Waterfall of Light

▶ **Answer each question. Give details from the story.**

1 Where does the story take place?

○ A. in a park   ○ C. at a waterfall

○ B. in the night   ○ D. on a folding chair

What helped you answer? _____

_____

_____

2 Why didn't Ming want to eat?

○ A. It was too cold.   ○ C. She didn't like noodles.

○ B. She was too excited.   ○ D. She was too sleepy.

What helped you answer? _____

_____

3 Why did people clap and shout that night?

_____

_____

_____

4 Explain the title of this story. _____

_____

_____

_____

_____

Literary Passages: Close Reading (Grade 2)
© 2016 Scholastic Inc.

Name _____ Date _____

The Orphan Train

Read the historical fiction story.

Then follow the directions in the Text Marking box.

Hannah stared out the window of a train heading west. She saw no houses, just endless flat land. The **prairie** seemed like a lonely place. Hannah felt weary. The eight-year-old had bounced on her hard train seat for three days.

Only days ago, Hannah was a homeless **orphan** living on the streets of New York City. She was rescued by people at the Children's Aid Society (suh-SYE-uh-tee). They put her on a train to go live with a farm family in Kansas. "They have room for you," she was told. In 1854, a child like her without parents was lucky to find a home anywhere. Hannah's future lay ahead, but she knew nothing of Kansas or farming. What if she didn't like the family? What if they disliked her?

Text Marking

Think about the setting and mood of the story.

☐ Draw a box around WHEN the story takes place.

⬭ Circle WHERE the story takes place.

___ Underline two details that set the mood.

Literary Passages: Close Reading (Grade 2)
© 2016 Scholastic Inc.

Name _____ Date _____

The Orphan Train

▶ **Answer each question. Give details from the story.**

1 What does the word **orphan** mean?

   ○ A. a child who does not have parents   ○ C. a farmer

   ○ B. a lost pet   ○ D. a homeless person

What helped you answer? _____

_____

_____

2 How do you think Hannah felt during the train ride?

   ○ A. hungry   ○ B. happy   ○ C. excited   ○ D. worried

What helped you answer? _____

_____

_____

_____

_____

3 Describe a **prairie**. _____

_____

_____

_____

_____

4 How does the setting of the story help set the mood?
Use another sheet of paper for your answer.

Literary Passages: Close Reading (Grade 2)
© 2016 Scholastic Inc.

Picnic for Three

Read the vacation story.

Then follow the directions in the Text Marking box.

Sasha, her dog, Petey, and her older cousin Mikel were in a rowboat one August afternoon. Mikel was rowing them to a nearby island for a picnic. It was a short boat ride away. A light breeze blew, and the sun was shining. The waves lapped gently against the boat.

Suddenly, the sun disappeared behind dark clouds, and everything changed. The gentle breeze became a wild wind that blew Sasha's hair and whipped at her clothes. The water became choppy and rocked the small boat from side to side. Then it began to pour.

"We must get back to shore," Mikel yelled. He rowed as hard as he could to reach safety. Petey barked and shook, so Sasha held him close. With her free hand, she gripped her seat tightly. The picnic would have to wait.

Text Marking

Think about the setting and mood of the story.

☐ Draw a box around WHEN the story takes place.

◯ Circle WHERE the story takes place.

_____ Underline three details that set the mood.

Name _____ Date _____

Picnic for Three

▶ **Answer each question. Give details from the story.**

1 When does the story take place?

   ○ A. during the night   ○ C. in the morning

   ○ B. during the day   ○ D. at lunch time

What helped you answer? _____

_____

2 What is the main reason the mood of the story changes?

   ○ A. Rain began to pour down.

   ○ B. Petey started barking.

   ○ C. Sasha and Mikel got too hungry to wait.

   ○ D. The weather went from calm to stormy.

What helped you answer? _____

_____

_____

_____

3 Describe what this sentence from the story means:
"The waves lapped gently against the boat."

_____

_____

_____

4 Explain the last sentence of the story. Use another sheet of paper.

Literary Passages: Close Reading (Grade 2)
© 2016 Scholastic Inc.

Name _____ Date _____

Rusty Stones

Read the science fiction story.

Then follow the directions in the Text Marking box.

Willa couldn't believe her eyes. There was a giant hole on her farm. Only the night before, tall corn had grown there. "What happened?" wondered Willa. She got off her tractor to explore the hole. Willa walked all the way around it. She saw packed dirt and rust-colored blobs of stone.

Slowly Willa stepped into the strange hole to grab a small stone. How heavy and warm it felt! Suddenly the stone began to jiggle in her hand. A squeaky voice cried, "KLEEP!" Willa looked more closely. She saw a crack that was bright purple inside. She noticed that the other rusty stones had the same look. They were also jiggling.

"What?" Willa thought. "Did a fleet of tiny spaceships crash into my farm?"

Text Marking

Think about the events in the story.

⬭ Circle two key events that happen.

___ Underline one detail about each event.

Literary Passages: Close Reading (Grade 2)
© 2016 Scholastic Inc.

Rusty Stones

▶ **Answer each question. Give details from the story.**

1 What surprised Willa first about the rusty stones?

  ○ A. They could speak. ○ C. They looked like spaceships.

  ○ B. They were heavy and warm. ○ D. They covered her cornfield.

  What helped you answer? _____

_____

_____

2 What did Willa think had happened at her farm?

  ○ A. Tiny spaceships had landed. ○ C. The corn turned purple.

  ○ B. There was a bad storm. ○ D. Her tractor broke down.

  What helped you answer? _____

_____

3 Look at the picture. Which part of the story does it show? Explain.

_____

_____

_____

4 A voice cried, "KLEEP!" What might that word mean?

_____

_____

_____

Literary Passages: Close Reading (Grade 2)
© 2016 Scholastic Inc.

Name _____   Date _____

Where's Frankie?

Read the mystery story.

Then follow the directions in the Text Marking box.

A funny thing happened one day when Ike went to feed Frankie. He was not in his tank or near it. Where did Ike's frog disappear to?

Ike put down the frog food to search for his missing pet. He looked in the kitchen and behind the couch in the living room. He searched under the beds in the bedrooms. He even opened all the closet doors and peeked in. No luck. Frankie was missing, and Ike was in tears.

"Now, THINK," Ike told himself, "What do frogs like? Where might Frankie want to be?" The lightbulb in Ike's head lit up brightly. He raced to the bathroom with a happy and knowing smile. There was Frankie in the tub by the drain. He seemed to be smiling, too.

Text Marking

Think about the events in the story.

◯ Circle two key events that happen.

___ <u>Underline</u> one detail about each event.

Literary Passages: Close Reading (Grade 2)
© 2016 Scholastic Inc.

Name _____ Date _____

Where's Frankie?

▶ **Answer each question. Give details from the mystery.**

1 Why did Ike cry?

○ A. Frankie was hungry.   ○ C. Frankie was lost.

○ B. Ike was hungry.   ○ D. Ike was lost.

What helped you answer? _____

_____

2 What does "the lightbulb in his head lit up brightly" mean?

○ A. Ike got a headache.   ○ C. Ike smiled from ear to ear.

○ B. Ike got a smart idea.   ○ D. Ike looked too long at the lamp.

What helped you answer? _____

_____

_____

3 What helped Ike figure out where to find Frankie?

_____

_____

_____

4 Retell the main events of the story in a few sentences.

_____

_____

_____

_____

Name _____ Date _____

Seeing the Seaport

Read the travel story.

Then follow the directions in the Text Marking box.

The Loh family entered the visitor center of the old seaport. There they planned their day. They picked out which activities, displays, and shows to see. They took a map of the seaport and began their tour.

First, the Lohs strolled all around the seaport. It looked as it did when it was filled with sailors, ship builders, and workers. Guides dressed the way people did 150 years ago. They told sailing stories. They sang sea songs. They worked on their crafts as visitors watched.

Next, the Lohs boarded three old sailing ships. Macey especially liked the wooden whale boat. Devin liked the old-fashioned fire boat. Mr. Loh said that visiting old ships can turn *landlubbers* into *sea dogs*.

★ Text Marking ★

Think about the events in the story.

⬭ Circle three key events on the Loh family's tour.

_____ Underline one detail about each event.

Literary Passages: Close Reading (Grade 2)
© 2016 Scholastic Inc.

Name _____ Date _____

Seeing the Seaport

▶ **Answer each question. Give details from the story.**

1 What did the Loh family do at the visitor center?

   ○ A. They sang whaling songs.   ○ C. They visited an old fire boat.

   ○ B. They turned into sea dogs.   ○ D. They decided which things to see.

   What helped you answer? _____

   _____

2 Who would rather NOT go to sea?

   ○ A. sea dogs   ○ B. landlubbers   ○ C. sailors   ○ D. guides

   What helped you answer? _____

   _____

   _____

   _____

   _____

3 Look at the picture. How does it help you understand the story?

   _____

   _____

   _____

4 Reread the last sentence of the story. What did Mr. Loh mean?

   _____

   _____

   _____

Literary Passages: Close Reading (Grade 2)
© 2016 Scholastic Inc.

A New Sitter

Read the realistic fiction story.

Then follow the directions in the Text Marking box.

Roxy rang the doorbell at 6 PM. She was the new babysitter. Tia frowned when Dad introduced them. "Where's Pam?" Tia grumbled. Pam was her usual sitter. Tia slumped onto the couch. She folded her arms across her chest and began to sulk.

After Tia's dad left, Roxy knew just what to do. She suggested making puppets together. Tia's frown turned into a smile. Tia and Roxy made paper-bag puppets. They used them to put on a silly play. The girls laughed and giggled all evening.

Tia's dad returned just before bedtime. "Dad, can Roxy be my sitter next time?" Tia asked. "She's the best!"

⭐ Text Marking ⭐

Find the sequence of events for Tia's evening.

☐ Draw boxes around the signal words **at 6 PM**, **after**, and **before bedtime**.

_____ <u>Underline</u> three important events.

1-2-3 Number the events in order.

Name _____ Date _____

A New Sitter

▶ **Answer each question. Give details from the story.**

1 Who was Pam?

○ A. the new babysitter   ○ C. the father

○ B. the old babysitter   ○ D. the child

What helped you answer? _____

_____

2 What happened in the middle of the story?

○ A. Roxy arrived at Tia's house.   ○ C. Tia and Roxy made puppets.

○ B. Tia sulked on the couch.   ○ D. Dad got home.

What helped you answer? _____

_____

_____

3 What made Tia change her mind about Roxy? Explain.

_____

_____

_____

4 What can you learn from this story about meeting new people?

_____

_____

_____

_____

Friends Play Putt-Putt

Read the sports story.

Then follow the directions in the Text Marking box.

Mom took Kai and Emily to Putt-Putt to play mini-golf. The first thing they did was to choose their golf **equipment**. Each picked a putter and a ball. Emily chose a yellow ball, and Kai took a blue one.

Next, they walked to the golf course and looked it over.

Then, Emily and Kai played the first hole. It was called Windmill. Kai went first and hit the ball with his putter. The ball hit the moving windmill and bounced back to him. Both kids laughed. Kai's second putt was better. He and Emily both got their balls into the hole in five tries. Emily kept track of their scores.

After they finished playing Windmill, the friends walked to the second hole. It was called Bridge. Emily went first this time. She aimed carefully at the narrow bridge…

★ Text Marking ★

Find the sequence of events at Putt-Putt.

☐   Draw boxes around the signal words **first**, **next**, **then**, and **after**.

___   Underline the most important events.

1-2-3-4   Number the events in order.

Literary Passages: Close Reading (Grade 2)
© 2016 Scholastic Inc.

Name _____ Date _____

Friends Play Putt-Putt

▶ **Answer each question. Give details from the story.**

1 Which piece of **equipment** did Kai and Emily pick?

○ A. a windmill   ○ B. a bridge   ○ C. a putter   ○ D. a hole

What helped you answer? _____

_____

2 When you "play a hole" in mini-golf, you _____.

○ A. putt the ball until you get it in the hole

○ B. putt the ball around the hole so it never falls in

○ C. play music as you walk the holes in the golf course

○ D. pretend to fall down and use the putter to get up

What helped you answer? _____

_____

3 Describe what Kai and Emily did BEFORE they played the Windmill hole.

_____

_____

_____

4 Predict: What do you think might happen when Emily plays the Bridge?

_____

_____

_____

_____

Literary Passages: Close Reading (Grade 2)
© 2016 Scholastic Inc.

Name _____   Date _____

Family Fun

Read the adventure story.

Then follow the directions in the Text Marking box.

The Perez family arrived at FunLand at 10 AM sharp. Mom paid the entrance fee and picked up tickets for rides. Excitement lay ahead!

After they skipped through the gates, they looked for the first ride to try. The colorful spinning teacups grabbed their attention. All four of them fit into one giant cup. "That was great!" Alonzo laughed. But the spinning made Luisa dizzy.

Next, they went to the bumper cars. Mom and Alonzo happily crashed about on this bumpy ride. Luisa and Dad watched and took photos. Luisa began to feel better.

Finally, they all rode the scary rollercoaster. Mom screamed the whole time, and Dad looked like a stone statue. But Alonzo and Luisa loved every speedy minute!

Text Marking

Find the sequence of events at FunLand.

☐ Draw boxes around the signal words and times.

___ Underline the most important events.

1-2-3-4 Number the events in order.

Literary Passages: Close Reading (Grade 2)
© 2016 Scholastic Inc.

Name _____ Date _____

Family Fun

▶ **Answer each question. Give details from the adventure.**

1 What was the third ride the Perez family went to?

   ○ A. the rollercoaster   ○ C. the entrance gate

   ○ B. the spinning teacups   ○ D. the bumper cars

What helped you answer? _____

_____

2 Why did Luisa watch with Dad at the bumper cars?

   ○ A. Luisa was scared of that ride.

   ○ B. Dad was too big for that ride.

   ○ C. She and Dad wanted something to eat.

   ○ D. Luisa was dizzy from the first ride.

What helped you answer? _____

_____

_____

3 How did the Perez family show that they knew "Excitement lay ahead"?

_____

_____

4 How did each member of the family react to the rollercoaster ride?

_____

_____

_____

Name _____   Date _____

Fishing for the Moon

Read the Chinese folktale.

Then follow the directions in the Text Marking box.

One clear night, Quan went to fetch water. He got a big surprise when he reached the village well. Deep down in the water was the moon. Its silvery face looked up at Quan.

"What a problem! Poor moon is stuck!" cried Quan as he raced home for his largest hook. He tied it to his bucket. Back at the well, he lowered the bucket to fish out the moon.

He jiggled the hook until he felt it catch. How he pulled and tugged! He yanked so hard that the rope on the bucket broke. Quan fell flat on his back. But when he looked up, the moon was back up high in the sky! Quan puffed up with pride. His plan had worked. He was the hero who rescued the moon.

★ Text Marking ★

Find the problem and Quan's solution.

☐ Draw boxes around the signal words **problem**, **plan**, and **rescued**.

◯ Circle the problem.

___ Underline Quan's solution.

Fishing for the Moon

▶ **Answer each question. Give details from the folktale.**

1 What surprise did Quan get at the village well?

○ A. He lost his hook.　　　○ C. There was no more water.

○ B. There was no bucket.　　○ D. The moon was stuck in the well.

What helped you answer? _____

_____

2 Which word means the same as **rescued**?

○ A. saved　　○ B. raced　　○ C. puffed up　　○ D. tugged

What helped you answer? _____

_____

_____

_____

3 Why did Quan go to the village that night?

_____

_____

4 Do you think Quan was a real hero? Explain.

_____

_____

_____

_____

_____

Literary Passages: Close Reading (Grade 2)

Name _____ Date _____

Bear Tale

Read the tall tale.

Then follow the directions in the Text Marking box.

Uncle Jake likes to tell a tale of trouble he found while exploring a cave in the woods. The problem was that he surprised a bear named Grizz. Grizz stood up tall and let out a mighty roar.

The first thought Uncle Jake had was to run. He ran as fast as he could. But Grizz ran after him and was catching up. Then Uncle Jake had a smart idea—he dropped his camera. That stopped Grizz in his tracks. Grizz grabbed the camera, took a selfie, and rolled over laughing.

> **Text Marking**
>
> Find the problem and the solutions.
>
> ▭ Draw boxes around the signal words.
>
> ⬭ Circle the problem.
>
> ___ Underline two solutions.

Grizz called Uncle Jake over to show him the photo. Uncle Jake laughed, too. That's how man and bear became pals. Whenever Uncle Jake is in those woods, he finds Grizz. They take pictures until they fall down giggling.

Literary Passages: Close Reading (Grade 2)
© 2016 Scholastic Inc.

Name _____ Date _____

Bear Tale

▶ **Answer each question. Give details from the tall tale.**

1 Where did Uncle Jake first come across Grizz?

○ A. in a zoo   ○ B. in a cave   ○ C. at a circus   ○ D. in his yard

What helped you answer? _____

_____

2 What was the first solution Uncle Jake tried?

○ A. He ran.   ○ C. He called for help.

○ B. He stood up tall.   ○ D. He gave a mighty roar.

What helped you answer? _____

_____

3 Why did Uncle Jake need a better solution? Explain.

_____

_____

_____

_____

4 Describe two or more clues that help you know this story is a tall tale.

_____

_____

_____

_____

Literary Passages: Close Reading (Grade 2)
© 2016 Scholastic Inc.

Ozzie's Goal

Read the circus story.

Then follow the directions in the Text Marking box.

Ozzie's dad performed in the circus. He did tricks on the high wire. He danced, walked backwards, and spun around up there and made it look easy! Ozzie admired his dad; he was his hero. But Ozzie didn't want to be exactly like him.

Ozzie's dream was to juggle. He set his heart on it. Dee-Dee the Clown helped by giving him beanbags to work with. Beanbags don't break or roll away when they drop. Dee-Dee used them to learn juggling herself. It was hard for Ozzie at first. But he practiced every day. Ozzie wanted to learn to juggle very much.

Text Marking

Use context clues to unlock the meaning of words.

◯ Circle the word **admired** and the sentence **He set his heart on it**.

___ Underline context clues for each.

After a month, Ozzie was juggling beanbags easily. "Soon you'll be juggling eggs!" Dee-Dee said with a wink. That did it—Ozzie had his next goal. He would get good enough to juggle raw eggs!

Literary Passages: Close Reading (Grade 2)
© 2016 Scholastic Inc.

Name _____ Date _____

Ozzie's Goal

▶ **Answer each question. Give details from the story.**

1 Another way to say **admired** is _____.

○ A. practiced   ○ B. looked up to   ○ C. got better   ○ D. feared

What helped you answer? _____

_____

2 Why did Ozzie practice juggling every day?

○ A. He wanted to make his dad proud of him.

○ B. He wanted to be a clown.

○ C. He wanted to become a good juggler.

○ D. It was the only thing he cared about.

What helped you answer? _____

_____

3 What do you do when you "set your heart on" something? Explain.

_____

_____

_____

_____

4 Why did Dee-Dee the Clown wink when she spoke about juggling eggs?

_____

_____

_____

Literary Passages: Close Reading (Grade 2)
© 2016 Scholastic Inc.

Name _____ Date _____

Holding Hands

Read the family story.

Then follow the directions in the Text Marking box.

Ellie, Dad, and her little brother Luke drove to the shopping mall. Ten-year-old Ellie sat in the back seat, safely wearing her seatbelt. But Luke was just two years old. He was tucked into his car seat beside her. Ellie kept turning her head around like an owl. She played "Peek-a-Boo" with Luke to hear his happy giggle.

After getting out of the car, Dad clutched Luke's right hand. The three walked toward the mall together. Luke's tiny hand disappeared into Dad's immense one. Ellie knew that Luke felt protected. Ellie remembered that secure feeling herself. She also used to hold her father's huge hand when she was learning to walk. She always knew Dad would keep her safe. She knew that Luke would be safe, too.

Text Marking

Use context clues to unlock the meanings of words.

◯ Circle the words **clutched** and **immense**.

___ Underline context clues for each word.

Literary Passages: Close Reading (Grade 2)
© 2016 Scholastic Inc.

Name _____ Date _____

Holding Hands

▶ **Answer each question. Give details from the story.**

1 Another word for **clutched** is _____.

○ A. wrapped   ○ B. washed   ○ C. rubbed   ○ D. held

What helped you answer? _____

_____

_____

2 What memory came to Ellie that day?

○ A. She remembered riding in a car seat.

○ B. She remembered learning to walk.

○ C. She remembered going to the mall.

○ D. She remembered what to buy at the mall.

What helped you answer? _____

_____

3 How does Ellie feel about her brother Luke? Explain.

_____

_____

_____

4 Look at the picture. How does it help you know the meaning of **immense**?

_____

_____

_____

Literary Passages: Close Reading (Grade 2)
© 2016 Scholastic Inc.

Name _____ Date _____

A Pair of Pots

Read the art story.

Then follow the directions in the Text Marking box.

Lamar loved working with clay. He took a pottery class in school. The last class was a pottery party. The students took turns describing two different pots they made. Lamar talked about his **coil pot** and his **slab pot**.

"For both pots, I used red clay that dries hard," said Lamar. "I used only my hands to make the coil pot. First I made a long clay snake. Then I coiled it around and around into a pot. I smoothed the inside to finish it.

"But for the slab pot, I used tools and my hands. I used a rolling pin to flatten the clay. I used a knife to cut five squares. I pieced them together into a pot. Then I smoothed all the seams."

Text Marking

Compare and contrast making coil pots and slab pots.

☐ Draw boxes around the signal words **both**, **only**, and **but**.

◯ Circle one way they are alike.

___ <u>Underline</u> one way they are different.

Literary Passages: Close Reading (Grade 2)
© 2016 Scholastic Inc.

Name _____ Date _____

A Pair of Pots

▶ **Answer each question. Give details from the story.**

1 How were Lamar's **coil pot** and **slab pot** alike?

○ A. Both were made of stone. ○ C. Both were made at pottery class.

○ B. Both were made with tools. ○ D. Both were made using only his hands.

What helped you answer? _____

_____

2 What did Lamar do FIRST to make his slab pot?

○ A. He flattened out the clay. ○ C. He smoothed out the seams.

○ B. He cut the clay into squares. ○ D. He let the pot dry until it was hard.

What helped you answer? _____

_____

3 Explain the main way that making coil pots is different from making slab pots.

_____

_____

_____

_____

4 Look at the picture. Use what Lamar said to tell what it shows.

_____

_____

_____

Name _____ Date _____

Spring Play

Read the theater story.

Then follow the directions in the Text Marking box.

Nikki, Meg, and Hari took part in the spring play at Pine Forest School. It was a musical set in a kingdom from long ago. Meg and Hari acted in the play. But Nikki took part in a different way. She was the **director**. She helped the actors do their best. Nikki told them where to stand, how to speak and sing, and how to move around the stage.

Meg starred as the king. She got to wear a shiny gold crown and a long purple robe. By contrast, Hari played a jester. He wore a pointy hat with bells. Nikki taught him a funny dance, which he learned quickly and well.

The play was a **hit**. The whole audience cheered at the end, so Meg, Hari, Nikki, and the others took five bows!

⭐ **Text Marking** ⭐

Compare and contrast what Nikki, Meg, and Hari did in the story.

☐ Draw boxes around the signal words **but**, **different** and **by contrast**.

⬭ Circle two things they did that was the same.

___ Underline things they did that were different.

Name _____ Date _____

Spring Play

▶ **Answer each question. Give details from the story.**

1 What is the job of a play's **director**?

○ A. to act in the play

○ B. to help the actors play their parts

○ C. to sing and dance

○ D. to sell tickets and hand out programs

What helped you answer? _____

_____

2 Who danced in the spring play?

○ A. Pine Forest School ○ B. Meg ○ C. Nikki ○ D. Hari

What helped you answer? _____

_____

3 What does it mean that the play was a **hit**?

_____

_____

_____

4 How were Meg and Hari's parts in the play alike?
How were they different?

_____

_____

_____

Answer Key

Sample Text Markings

---

1 Character   Name _____   Date _____

Dancing Day

Read the dance story.
Then follow the directions in the Text Marking box.

(Zoey) was walking home from school with her friend Trey. She had an extra bounce in her step.

"Why are you so jiggly and bubbly today?" asked Trey.

"It's Wednesday," said Zoey. "This is my favorite day. It's when I go to my dance class. My friend Max's mom teaches us. She used to be a dancer. We practice in their basement."

She gave her backpack to Trey to hold. Then she did a graceful leap and twirl right there in the middle of the sidewalk. Trey smiled, gave her a "thumbs up," and said, "Look at you, girl!"

"Why don't you come along with me," she said. "It's really fun to dance!"

★ Text Marking

Think about the story.

◯   Circle WHO the story is mostly about.

___   Underline two details that tell about that person.

14

◀ Sample Text Markings

Passage 1: Dancing Day

1. C; Sample answer: I picked C because he asks Zoey why she is acting so jiggly and bubbly, and that's like bouncing around.

2. B; Sample answer: I picked B because I found those words in the story and read that Zoey said them.

3. Sample answer: I think she wanted to show how much fun she has when she dances.

4. Accept reasonable responses. Sample answers: He and Zoey are friends, so maybe he'll give it a try. Or: Maybe Zoey first has to ask Max's mom if she can bring another student to the class.

---

2 Character   Name _____   Date _____

Satellite Search

Read the historical fiction story.
Then follow the directions in the Text Marking box.

It was October, 1957. (Nora) and (Fred) went to bed early because they would lose sleep later. (Fred) fussed about the babyish bedtime. (Fred) didn't care about science. (Nora) was different. She knew about Sputnik (SPUHT-nik). She knew it was the first satellite (SAT-uh-lite) ever to travel around Earth. She had heard this spacecraft's "beep-beep" sound on the radio. She saw photos and read news stories about it.

That night, the whole family went outside after midnight. They searched the dark sky for Sputnik. "Is that it?" (Nora) asked, pointing to a bright star.

"No," said Dad. "Sputnik moves fast, like a shooting star."

"Can't I go to sleep?" whined (Fred)

"No! Keep looking!" (Nora) urged.

Mom spotted it first, pointing, "I think that's Sputnik!

"Freddie, look!" cried (Nora) But her brother was already sound asleep on the grass.

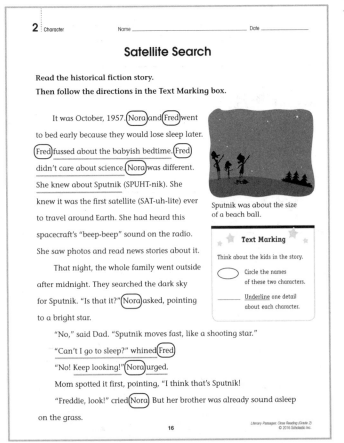

Sputnik was about the size of a beach ball.

★ Text Marking ★

Think about the kids in the story.

◯   Circle the names of these two characters.

___   Underline one detail about each character.

16

◀ Sample Text Markings

Passage 2: Satellite Search

1. C; Sample answer: I picked C because the story said so in the first paragraph.

2. A; Sample answer: The story showed that she is interested in science and that she knew about Sputnik.

3. Sample answers: Their parents would wake the kids up in the middle of the night to go outside to look for Sputnik.

4. Sample answers: It says at the beginning that it was October in 1957. That is many years ago!

Name _____ Date _____

Fox and Stork

Read the fable.
Then follow the directions in the Text Marking box.

One day (Fox) made soup. As it cooked, (Stork) flew by. That gave Fox a sly idea. He invited Stork to join him for soup. "Come back at dark, Stork."

"How kind," Stork thought. But Fox planned a mean trick.

Later, Fox served bowls of soup. But Stork's bowl was too shallow for her long beak. She could not taste one drop. Fox slurped loudly and said, "Mmmm, yummy!" Poor Stork felt hungry and insulted. Still, she asked Fox to eat with her the next night. Fox agreed.

Fox went to Stork's home for dinner. Stork served fish stew in tall skinny jars. Stork's pointy beak fit nicely, and she ate her fill. But Fox could not taste one drop. He went home hungry and angry.

Text Marking

Think about the fable.

◯ Circle the name of each character.

___ Underline two details about each character.

18

Literary Passages: Close Reading (Grade 2)
© 2016 Scholastic Inc.

◀ Sample Text Markings

Passage 3: Fox and Stork

1. A; Sample answer: I picked A because the story said so in the first paragraph.

2. D; Sample answer: In this story, the fox tricked the stork about dinner, and she tricked him the next day in the same way.

3. Sample answers: He didn't have a long beak that could fit into the tall skinny jar she served it in.

4. Sample answers: I think he did that to make fun of Stork having trouble eating from the shallow bowl.

Name _____ Date _____

Bart's Spider Scare

Read the nature story.
Then follow the directions in the Text Marking box.

[Bart] was in the garden when he spotted a scary, hairy spider. He began shouting, ("A spider, a spider! Kill it quick!")

"Calm down," called [Grandpa] from the porch. "What's all the **fuss**?"

Bart told Grandpa about the spider. He led Grandpa to the garden for a look.

"Now that is a welcome sight," said Grandpa. "This spider will eat insects that could harm my plants, so I'm glad it's here." Then he said, "Welcome to my garden, spider!"

("But…I thought spiders were bad,") said Bart. ("Don't they bite? Don't they have poison?")

"Some spiders can hurt people, but many are helpful," said Grandpa. "It pays to learn about nature. Then you will know which animals to stay away from. You will also know a friend when you spot one!"

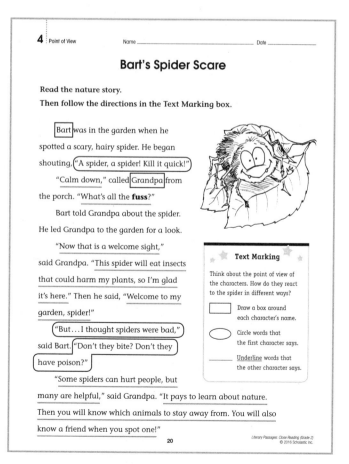

Text Marking

Think about the point of view of the characters. How do they react to the spider in different ways?

▢ Draw a box around each character's name.

◯ Circle words that the first character says.

___ Underline words that the other character says.

20

Literary Passages: Close Reading (Grade 2)
© 2016 Scholastic Inc.

◀ Sample Text Markings

Passage 4: Bart's Spider Scare

1. C; Sample answer: I picked C because Bart wasn't quiet at all when he was shouting about the spider.

2. D; Sample answer: I picked D because those marks are used to show words a character says.

3. Sample answer: Grandpa wasn't afraid of the spider. He knew it would be helpful to his garden.

4. Sample answer: Bart shouts that he wants the spider dead because he is afraid of it and thinks spiders are bad. But Grandpa knows that spiders are good for his garden and is happy to see the spider.

Name _____ Date _____

Up the Elephant's Trunk
by Kirk Mann

Read the poem.
Then follow the directions in the Text Marking box.

The (elephant) once said to me,
"Mouse, please climb in my nose
And go until I say to stop,
Then scratch there with your toes."

I climbed inside the long, deep trunk,
The air was damp and gray.
I walked across some peanut shells
And grass and bits of hay.

Then halfway up the bumpy trail
The elephant yelled, "Stop!"
"Scratch," he said, "with all your might,
And jump and kick and hop."

I scratched and itched and itched and scratched.
He finally yelled, "Enough!"
And then he blew me out his trunk
With lots of other stuff!

★ ★ **Text Marking** ★ ★

Each character in the poem
has a point of view.

☐ Draw a box around
the narrator.

◯ Circle the character
that wants help.

___ Underline what the
narrator does to help.

22

Literary Passages: Close Reading (Grade 2)
© 2016 Scholastic Inc.

◀ Sample Text Markings

Passage 5: Up the Elephant's Trunk

1. B; Sample answer: I picked B because that's why he asks the mouse for help.

2. D; Sample answer: The poem made me picture the mouse climbing inside the long, deep trunk and described what he did in there.

3. Sample answer: It describes the inside of the elephant's long trunk.

4. Sample answer: The mouse is kind and helpful, and doesn't complain. He does what the elephant asks.

Name _____ Date _____

Waterfall of Light

Read the holiday story.
Then follow the directions in the Text Marking box.

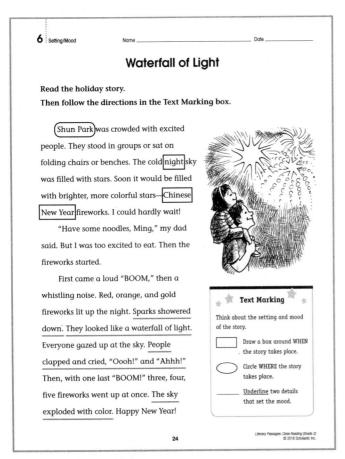

(Shun Park) was crowded with excited people. They stood in groups or sat on folding chairs or benches. The cold night sky was filled with stars. Soon it would be filled with brighter, more colorful stars—Chinese New Year fireworks. I could hardly wait!

"Have some noodles, Ming," my dad said. But I was too excited to eat. Then the fireworks started.

First came a loud "BOOM," then a whistling noise. Red, orange, and gold fireworks lit up the night. Sparks showered down. They looked like a waterfall of light. Everyone gazed up at the sky. People clapped and cried, "Oooh!" and "Ahhh!" Then, with one last "BOOM!" three, four, five fireworks went up at once. The sky exploded with color. Happy New Year!

★ ★ **Text Marking** ★ ★

Think about the setting and mood
of the story.

☐ Draw a box around WHEN
the story takes place.

◯ Circle WHERE the story
takes place.

___ Underline two details
that set the mood.

24

Literary Passages: Close Reading (Grade 2)
© 2016 Scholastic Inc.

◀ Sample Text Markings

Passage 6: Waterfall of Light

1. A; Sample answer: I picked A because the story says, "Shun Park was crowded with excited people."

2. B; Sample answer: I picked B because it said that in the middle of the story.

3. Sample answer: I think they really enjoyed the fireworks show.

4. Sample answer: When the fireworks exploded, bright colorful sparks of light fell down from the sky. They kept coming down, like the water in a waterfall.

Literary Passages: Close Reading (Grade 2)
© 2016 Scholastic Inc.

Name _____ Date _____

The Orphan Train

Read the historical fiction story.
Then follow the directions in the Text Marking box.

Hannah stared out the window of a (train) heading west. She saw no houses, just endless flat land. The **prairie** seemed like a lonely place. Hannah felt weary. The eight-year-old had bounced on her hard train seat for three days.

Only days ago, Hannah was a homeless **orphan** living on the streets of New York City. She was rescued by people at the Children's Aid Society (suh-SYE-uh-tee). They put her on a train to go live with a farm family in Kansas. "They have room for you," she was told. In 1854, a child like her without parents was lucky to find a home anywhere. Hannah's future lay ahead, but she knew nothing of Kansas or farming. What if she didn't like the family? What if they disliked her?

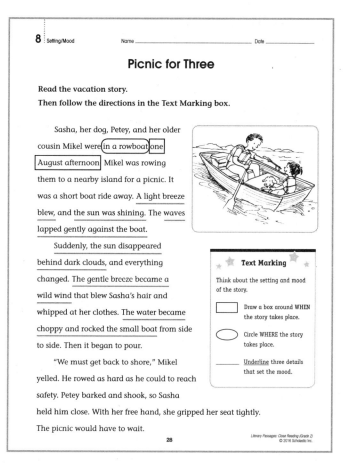

> ★ **Text Marking** ★
>
> Think about the setting and mood of the story.
>
> ▢ Draw a box around WHEN the story takes place.
>
> ◯ Circle WHERE the story takes place.
>
> ___ Underline two details that set the mood.

26

Literary Passages: Close Reading (Grade 2)
© 2016 Scholastic Inc.

◀ Sample Text Markings

Passage 7: The Orphan Train

1. A; I picked A because the second paragraph says that Hannah was an orphan. Then it says "a child like her without parents."

2. D; Sample answer: I think Hannah was worried because she was taking a long trip by herself across the country and didn't know anything about Kansas or farming or if she and her new family would like each other.

3. The story says that a prairie is flat, empty land in the west that goes on and on. It also says that Hannah is going to live with a farm family in Kansas, so the prairie might have farmland.

4. The author says Hannah thought the prairie seemed like a lonely place. Besides being worried about her new life, I think she felt lonely, too. And she had been travelling alone on a train for days, so that would be lonesome, too.

Name _____ Date _____

Picnic for Three

Read the vacation story.
Then follow the directions in the Text Marking box.

Sasha, her dog, Petey, and her older cousin Mikel were in a rowboat one August afternoon. Mikel was rowing them to a nearby island for a picnic. It was a short boat ride away. A light breeze blew, and the sun was shining. The waves lapped gently against the boat.

Suddenly, the sun disappeared behind dark clouds, and everything changed. The gentle breeze became a wild wind that blew Sasha's hair and whipped at her clothes. The water became choppy and rocked the small boat from side to side. Then it began to pour.

"We must get back to shore," Mikel yelled. He rowed as hard as he could to reach safety. Petey barked and shook, so Sasha held him close. With her free hand, she gripped her seat tightly. The picnic would have to wait.

> ★ **Text Marking** ★
>
> Think about the setting and mood of the story.
>
> ▢ Draw a box around WHEN the story takes place.
>
> ◯ Circle WHERE the story takes place.
>
> ___ Underline three details that set the mood.

28

Literary Passages: Close Reading (Grade 2)
© 2016 Scholastic Inc.

◀ Sample Text Markings

Passage 8: Picnic for Three

1. B; Sample answer: I picked B because the story says, "one August afternoon."

2. D; Sample answer: I picked D because at first it's a really nice sunny day and they're going to have a fun picnic. But when the weather gets stormy, the mood gets dangerous and kind of scary.

3. Sample answer: I think it means that they could feel the waves gently bumping into the boat.

4. Sample answer: The sudden storm meant that they couldn't keep rowing to the island for the picnic. It was more important to get back to shore safely.

Rusty Stones

Read the science fiction story.
Then follow the directions in the Text Marking box.

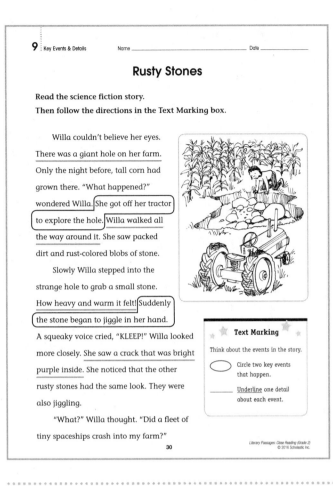

Willa couldn't believe her eyes. There was a giant hole on her farm. Only the night before, tall corn had grown there. "What happened?" wondered Willa. She got off her tractor to explore the hole. Willa walked all the way around it. She saw packed dirt and rust-colored blobs of stone.

Slowly Willa stepped into the strange hole to grab a small stone. How heavy and warm it felt! Suddenly the stone began to jiggle in her hand. A squeaky voice cried, "KLEEP!" Willa looked more closely. She saw a crack that was bright purple inside. She noticed that the other rusty stones had the same look. They were also jiggling.

"What?" Willa thought. "Did a fleet of tiny spaceships crash into my farm?"

Text Marking

Think about the events in the story.

◯ Circle two key events that happen.

___ Underline one detail about each event.

30

Literary Passages: Close Reading (Grade 2)
© 2016 Scholastic Inc.

Passage 9: Rusty Stones

1. B; Sample answer: I picked B because that's what it said in the second paragraph.

2. A; Sample answer: I picked A because in the last sentence of the story, it says that's what Willa thought.

3. Sample answer: I think it shows the beginning, when Willa got off her tractor and went to look at the big hole.

4. Sample answer: It might mean "Help" or be a warning like, "Stay away!"

Where's Frankie?

Read the mystery story.
Then follow the directions in the Text Marking box.

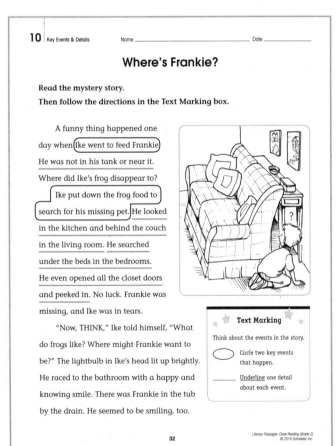

A funny thing happened one day when Ike went to feed Frankie. He was not in his tank or near it. Where did Ike's frog disappear to? Ike put down the frog food to search for his missing pet. He looked in the kitchen and behind the couch in the living room. He searched under the beds in the bedrooms. He even opened all the closet doors and peeked in. No luck. Frankie was missing, and Ike was in tears.

"Now, THINK," Ike told himself, "What do frogs like? Where might Frankie want to be?" The lightbulb in Ike's head lit up brightly. He raced to the bathroom with a happy and knowing smile. There was Frankie in the tub by the drain. He seemed to be smiling, too.

Text Marking

Think about the events in the story.

◯ Circle two key events that happen.

___ Underline one detail about each event.

32

Literary Passages: Close Reading (Grade 2)
© 2016 Scholastic Inc.

Passage 10: Where's Frankie?

1. C; Sample answer: I picked C because Ike was upset that he couldn't find Frankie.

2. B; Sample answer: I picked B because Ike used his brain to think about where Ike might be. A bright lightbulb is like a bright idea.

3. Sample answer: Ike tried to think about where a frog would want to be. Frogs like water, so Ike checked the bathroom.

4. Sample answer: Ike's frog Frankie wasn't in his tank. Ike looked all over for him. He finally found Frankie in the bathtub.

Passage 11: Seeing the Seaport

1. D; Sample answer: I picked D because that's the only thing that happened at the visitor center.

2. B; Sample answer: I picked B because it sounds like "land lovers." Also, if a visit to a seaport can turn landlubbers into sea dogs then a landlubber probably is not someone who likes the sea to begin with.

3. Sample answer: I see how big and fancy an old whaling ship was, and can imagine how different that old ship looks compared to modern ships.

4. Sample answer: I think he meant that people might want to go sailing after learning so much at the old seaport.

Passage 12: A New Sitter

1. B; Sample answer: I picked B because I figured that out from the first paragraph.

2. C; Sample answer: I picked C because that's what happened between the beginning and the end.

3. Sample answer: Tia didn't expect to like Roxy, but Roxy came up with a fun project, and they had a good time together.

4. Sample answer: Give them a chance. Get to know them before you judge them.

The left side of the page shows two worksheet reproductions:

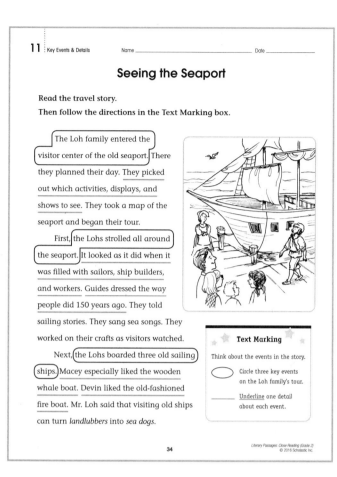

11 Key Events & Details   Name _____   Date _____

Seeing the Seaport

Read the travel story.
Then follow the directions in the Text Marking box.

The Loh family entered the visitor center of the old seaport. There they planned their day. They picked out which activities, displays, and shows to see. They took a map of the seaport and began their tour.

First, the Lohs strolled all around the seaport. It looked as it did when it was filled with sailors, ship builders, and workers. Guides dressed the way people did 150 years ago. They told sailing stories. They sang sea songs. They worked on their crafts as visitors watched.

Next, the Lohs boarded three old sailing ships. Macey especially liked the wooden whale boat. Devin liked the old-fashioned fire boat. Mr. Loh said that visiting old ships can turn *landlubbers* into *sea dogs*.

★ Text Marking ★

Think about the events in the story.

⬭ Circle three key events on the Loh family's tour.

___ Underline one detail about each event.

34

Literary Passages: Close Reading (Grade 2)
© 2016 Scholastic Inc.

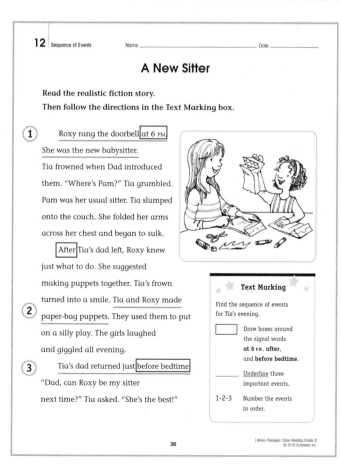

12 Sequence of Events   Name _____   Date _____

A New Sitter

Read the realistic fiction story.
Then follow the directions in the Text Marking box.

1 Roxy rang the doorbell at 6 PM. She was the new babysitter. Tia frowned when Dad introduced them. "Where's Pam?" Tia grumbled. Pam was her usual sitter. Tia slumped onto the couch. She folded her arms across her chest and began to sulk.

After Tia's dad left, Roxy knew just what to do. She suggested making puppets together. Tia's frown turned into a smile. Tia and Roxy made **2** paper-bag puppets. They used them to put on a silly play. The girls laughed and giggled all evening.

3 Tia's dad returned just before bedtime. "Dad, can Roxy be my sitter next time?" Tia asked. "She's the best!"

★ Text Marking ★

Find the sequence of events for Tia's evening.

☐ Draw boxes around the signal words **at 6 PM, after,** and **before bedtime.**

___ Underline three important events.

1-2-3 Number the events in order.

36

Literary Passages: Close Reading (Grade 2)
© 2016 Scholastic Inc.

Friends Play Putt-Putt

Read the sports story.
Then follow the directions in the Text Marking box.

① Mom took Kai and Emily to Putt-Putt to play mini-golf. The first thing they did was to choose their golf **equipment**. Each picked a putter and a ball. Emily chose a yellow ball, and Kai took a blue one.

② Next, they walked to the golf course and looked it over.

③ Then, Emily and Kai played the first hole. It was called Windmill. Kai went first and hit the ball with his putter. The ball hit the moving windmill and bounced back to him. Both kids laughed. Kai's second putt was better. He and Emily both got their balls into the hole in five tries. Emily kept track of their scores.

④ After they finished playing Windmill, the friends walked to the second hole. It was called Bridge. Emily went first this time. She aimed carefully at the narrow bridge…

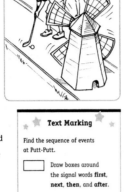

Text Marking

Find the sequence of events at Putt-Putt.

☐ Draw boxes around the signal words **first**, **next**, **then**, and **after**.

___ Underline the most important events.

1-2-3-4 Number the events in order.

38

Literary Passages: Close Reading (Grade 2)
© 2016 Scholastic Inc.

◀ Sample Text Markings

Passage 13: Friends Play Putt-Putt

1. C; Sample answer: In the first paragraph, it says they each picked a putter. The other things are parts of the mini-golf course.

2. A; Sample answer: In paragraph 3, it says that both kids got their balls in the hole after five tries.

3. Sample answer: They chose their putter and ball first, then they went to the course and looked it over.

4. Accept reasonable responses. Sample answer: The ball might hit the bridge and bounce back like Kai's did. But if Emily aims well, it might go over the bridge and end up near the hole.

Family Fun

Read the adventure story.
Then follow the directions in the Text Marking box.

① The Perez family arrived at FunLand at 10 AM sharp. Mom paid the entrance fee and picked up tickets for rides. Excitement lay ahead!

② After they skipped through the gates, they looked for the first ride to try. The colorful spinning teacups grabbed their attention. All four of them fit into one giant cup. "That was great!" Alonzo laughed. But the spinning made Luisa dizzy.

③ Next, they went to the bumper cars. Mom and Alonzo happily crashed about on this bumpy ride. Luisa and Dad watched and took photos. Luisa began to feel better.

④ Finally, they all rode the scary rollercoaster. Mom screamed the whole time, and Dad looked like a stone statue. But Alonzo and Luisa loved every speedy minute!

Text Marking

Find the sequence of events at FunLand.

☐ Draw boxes around the signal words and times.

___ Underline the most important events.

1-2-3-4 Number the events in order.

40

Literary Passages: Close Reading (Grade 2)
© 2016 Scholastic Inc.

◀ Sample Text Markings

Passage 14: Family Fun

1. A; Sample answer: I picked A because I counted off the rides. First they did the teacups, next they did the bumper cars, then the rollercoaster.

2. D; Sample answer: I picked D because Luisa got dizzy on the first ride, and probably wanted to wait until she felt better.

3. Sample answer: They skipped through the gates which showed that they were happy and eager to get to the rides.

4. Sample answer: Alonzo and Luisa loved it, but Mom and Dad acted nervous and scared.

Ozzie's Goal

Read the circus story.
Then follow the directions in the Text Marking box.

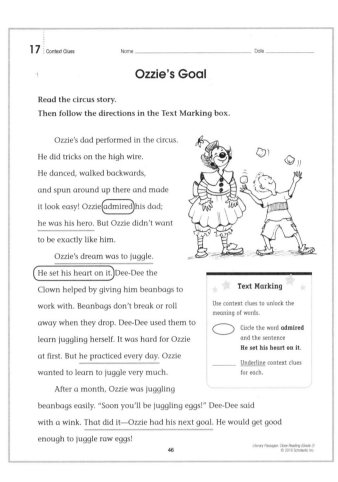

Ozzie's dad performed in the circus. He did tricks on the high wire. He danced, walked backwards, and spun around up there and made it look easy! Ozzie (admired) his dad; he was his hero. But Ozzie didn't want to be exactly like him.

Ozzie's dream was to juggle. (He set his heart on it.) Dee-Dee the Clown helped by giving him beanbags to work with. Beanbags don't break or roll away when they drop. Dee-Dee used them to learn juggling herself. It was hard for Ozzie at first. But he practiced every day. Ozzie wanted to learn to juggle very much.

After a month, Ozzie was juggling beanbags easily. "Soon you'll be juggling eggs!" Dee-Dee said with a wink. That did it—Ozzie had his next goal. He would get good enough to juggle raw eggs!

★ **Text Marking** ★

Use context clues to unlock the meaning of words.

◯ Circle the word **admired** and the sentence **He set his heart on it.**

___ Underline context clues for each.

46

Literary Passages: Close Reading (Grade 2)
© 2016 Scholastic Inc.

Holding Hands

Read the family story.
Then follow the directions in the Text Marking box.

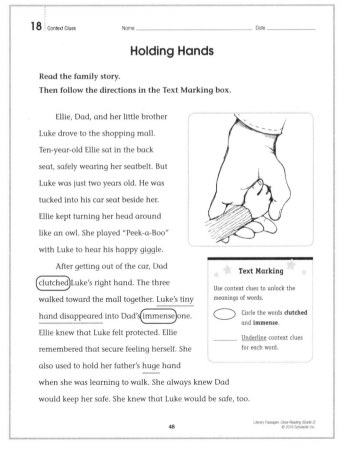

Ellie, Dad, and her little brother Luke drove to the shopping mall. Ten-year-old Ellie sat in the back seat, safely wearing her seatbelt. But Luke was just two years old. He was tucked into his car seat beside her. Ellie kept turning her head around like an owl. She played "Peek-a-Boo" with Luke to hear his happy giggle.

After getting out of the car, Dad (clutched) Luke's right hand. The three walked toward the mall together. Luke's tiny hand disappeared into Dad's (immense) one. Ellie knew that Luke felt protected. Ellie remembered that secure feeling herself. She also used to hold her father's huge hand when she was learning to walk. She always knew Dad would keep her safe. She knew that Luke would be safe, too.

★ **Text Marking** ★

Use context clues to unlock the meanings of words.

◯ Circle the words **clutched** and **immense.**

___ Underline context clues for each word.

48

Literary Passages: Close Reading (Grade 2)
© 2016 Scholastic Inc.

◀ Sample Text Markings

Passage 17: Ozzie's Goal

1. B; Sample answer: I picked B because Ozzie's dad is his hero, so he looks up to him.

2. C; Sample answer: I picked C because juggling is hard, so if you want to learn it, you must practice.

3. Sample answer: When you set your heart on something, you really want it. You work hard to make it happen. In the story, Ozzie set his heart on learning to juggle. That's what he wanted. That was his goal.

4. Sample answer: Dee-Dee knew that eggs break if you drop them and jugglers do drop things as they learn. Ozzie is getting better, but has a way to go before he can juggle raw eggs.

◀ Sample Text Markings

Passage 18: Holding Hands

1. D; Sample answer: I picked D because the picture shows the dad holding little Luke's hand. Also, near the end of the story I read that Ellie used to hold her father's hand, too.

2. B; Sample answer: I picked B because the story says this in the second paragraph.

3. Sample answer: Ellie likes making Luke laugh which shows that she cares about him. She also understands how important it is to keep him safe.

4. Sample answer: *Immense* means big. The picture shows a little child's hand beside a large adult hand.

15 Problem & Solution   Name _____ Date _____

Fishing for the Moon

Read the Chinese folktale.
Then follow the directions in the Text Marking box.

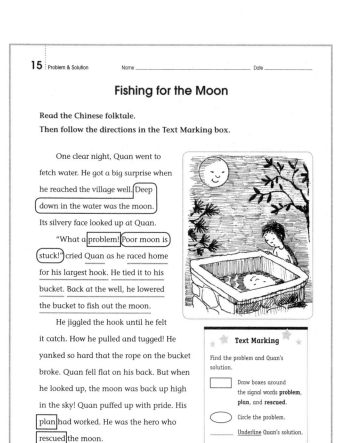

One clear night, Quan went to fetch water. He got a big surprise when he reached the village well. Deep down in the water was the moon. Its silvery face looked up at Quan.

"What a problem! Poor moon is stuck!" cried Quan as he raced home for his largest hook. He tied it to his bucket. Back at the well, he lowered the bucket to fish out the moon.

He jiggled the hook until he felt it catch. How he pulled and tugged! He yanked so hard that the rope on the bucket broke. Quan fell flat on his back. But when he looked up, the moon was back up high in the sky! Quan puffed up with pride. His plan had worked. He was the hero who rescued the moon.

★ **Text Marking** ★

Find the problem and Quan's solution.

▭ Draw boxes around the signal words **problem**, **plan**, and **rescued**.

⬭ Circle the problem.

___ Underline Quan's solution.

42

Literary Passages: Close Reading (Grade 2)
© 2016 Scholastic Inc.

Passage 15: Fishing for the Moon

1. D; Sample answer: I picked D because the story says this in the first paragraph.

2. A; Sample answer: I picked A because Quan thought he had saved the moon from being stuck in the well.

3. Sample answer: He needed water from the well there.

4. Sample answer: No, I don't think Quan was a hero. He believed the moon was really in the well, but it was just a reflection. The moon was in the sky all along, but Quan never noticed it. So he really didn't rescue anything.

---

16 Problem & Solution   Name _____ Date _____

Bear Tale

Read the tall tale.
Then follow the directions in the Text Marking box.

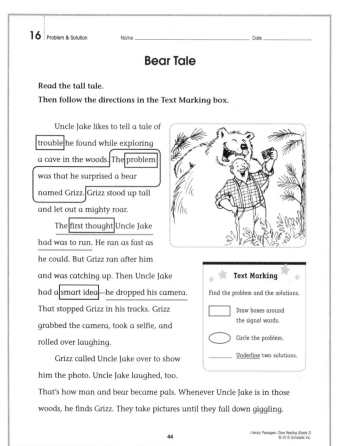

Uncle Jake likes to tell a tale of trouble he found while exploring a cave in the woods. The problem was that he surprised a bear named Grizz. Grizz stood up tall and let out a mighty roar.

The first thought Uncle Jake had was to run. He ran as fast as he could. But Grizz ran after him and was catching up. Then Uncle Jake had a smart idea—he dropped his camera. That stopped Grizz in his tracks. Grizz grabbed the camera, took a selfie, and rolled over laughing.

Grizz called Uncle Jake over to show him the photo. Uncle Jake laughed, too. That's how man and bear became pals. Whenever Uncle Jake is in those woods, he finds Grizz. They take pictures until they fall down *giggling*.

★ **Text Marking** ★

Find the problem and the solutions.

▭ Draw boxes around the signal words.

⬭ Circle the problem.

___ Underline two solutions.

44

Literary Passages: Close Reading (Grade 2)
© 2016 Scholastic Inc.

Passage 16: Bear Tale

1. B; Sample answer: I picked B because the story says this in the first paragraph.

2. A; Sample answer: I picked A because the story says that in paragraph 2.

3. Sample answer: He couldn't run fast or far enough to get away from Grizz. So he had to think of something else, and FAST!

4. Sample answer: Bears don't know how to use cameras or take selfies, they don't laugh, and they don't make friends with people.

A Pair of Pots

Read the art story.
Then follow the directions in the Text Marking box.

Lamar loved working with clay. He took a pottery class in school. The last class was a pottery party. The students took turns describing two different pots they made. Lamar talked about his **coil pot** and his **slab pot**.

"For both pots, I used red clay that dries hard," said Lamar. "I used only my hands to make the coil pot. First I made a long clay snake. Then I coiled it around and around into a pot. I smoothed the inside to finish it.

"But for the slab pot, I used tools and my hands. I used a rolling pin to flatten the clay. I used a knife to cut five squares. I pieced them together into a pot. Then I smoothed all the seams."

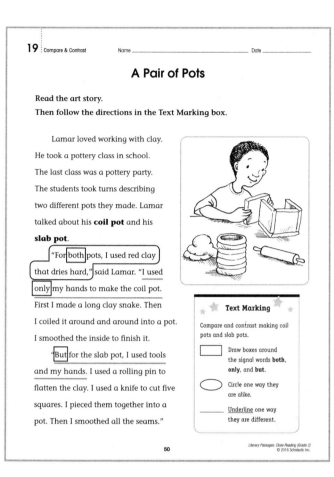

Text Marking

Compare and contrast making coil pots and slab pots.

▢ Draw boxes around the signal words **both**, **only**, and **but**.

◯ Circle one way they are alike.

___ Underline one way they are different.

50

Literary Passages: Close Reading (Grade 2)
© 2016 Scholastic Inc.

Passage 19: A Pair of Pots

1. C; Sample answer: I picked C because it is the only statement that is true.

2. A; Sample answer: I picked A because Lamar said that in his talk.

3. Sample answer: For a coil pot, you use your hands to make a long snake of clay and wind it around into a pot shape. For a slab pot, you use tools to flatten and then cut the clay into large flat pieces that you put together to form a pot.

4. Sample answer: The boy is working on the slab pot, putting flat pieces together. But it also shows a round coil pot, with the coiled outside.

Spring Play

Read the theater story.
Then follow the directions in the Text Marking box.

Nikki, Meg, and Hari took part in the spring play at Pine Forest School. It was a musical set in a kingdom from long ago. Meg and Hari acted in the play. But Nikki took part in a different way. She was the **director**. She helped the actors do their best. Nikki told them where to stand, how to speak and sing, and how to move around the stage.

Meg starred as the king. She got to wear a shiny gold crown and a long purple robe. By contrast, Hari played a jester. He wore a pointy hat with bells. Nikki taught him a funny dance, which he learned quickly and well.

The play was a **hit**. The whole audience cheered at the end, so Meg, Hari, Nikki, and the others took five bows!

Text Marking

Compare and contrast what Nikki, Meg, and Hari did in the story.

▢ Draw boxes around the signal words **but**, **different** and **by contrast**.

◯ Circle two things they did that was the same.

___ Underline things they did that were different.

52

Literary Passages: Close Reading (Grade 2)
© 2016 Scholastic Inc.

Passage 20: Spring Play

1. B; Sample answer: I picked B because in the first paragraph it says that Nikki helped the actors do their best.

2. D; Sample answer: I picked D because Hari was the jester who did a funny dance.

3. Sample answer: It says in the last paragraph that everyone cheered and the actors took five bows, so I think it means that people really liked it a lot.

4. Sample answer: Both kids acted in the play. But Meg was the king. Hari was a jester. He also did a funny dance.

Notes